WHAT IT MEANS TO BE
SERIES

PUBLISHER	Joseph R. DeVarennes
PUBLICATION DIRECTOR	Kenneth H. Pearson
ADVISORS	Roger Aubin
	Robert Furlonger
EDITORIAL MANAGER	Jocelyn Smyth
EDITORS	Ann Martin
	Shelley McGuinness
	Robin Rivers
	Mayta Tannenbaum
ARTISTS	Summer Morse
	Barbara Pileggi
	Steve Pileggi
	Mike Stearns
PRODUCTION MANAGER	Ernest Homewood
PRODUCTION ASSISTANTS	Catherine Gordon
	Kathy Kishimoto
PUBLICATION ADMINISTRATOR	Anna Good

Canadian Cataloguing in Publication Data

Zola, Melanie, 1952-
  What it means to be—generous

(What it means to be; 14)
ISBN 0-7172-2240-3

1. Generosity — Juvenile literature.
I. Pileggi, Steve.   II. Title.   III. Title: Generous.   IV. Series.

BJ1533.G4Z64   1987   j177'.7   C87-095056-8

WHAT IT MEANS TO BE...

GENEROUS

Written by

Melanie Zola

Illustrated by

Steve Pileggi

Generous people make everybody feel welcome.

Joey and Eva were sitting on her front porch cutting pictures out of old magazines. They were each making a collage. After they had collected a large pile of clippings, they set them out on two pieces of construction paper making sure to overlap the edges.

Hannah was walking along the sidewalk feeling lonely. She had no one to play with. When she saw Joey and Eva, she stopped to watch them.

Joey noticed her. "Hi, Hannah," he said.

"What are you doing?" she asked. She walked across Eva's front lawn to take a better look.

"We're making collages," Eva answered. "Would you like to try?"

Hannah's eyes lit up. "Oh, yes!"

You can help someone who is alone feel better by inviting him or her to join you. Sharing your time with others is a generous thing to do.

Being generous with thanks is important.

Hannah sat down with Joey and Eva. They pushed the magazines toward her.

"First, you cut out everything you want to put in your collage," explained Joey.

"You can layer the clippings to make an interesting design," added Eva.

Hannah listened carefully and then started cutting. Eva helped her with the glue.

"Just put on enough glue so the pictures stick to the paper," Eva advised.

They talked and laughed as they cut and glued. Soon the three collages were complete. Joey's had animals running and crawling all over it. Eva's had faces of different sizes and colors. Hannah's collage was filled with every type of food imaginable.

When it was time for Hannah to go home, she said, "Thank you for asking me to play. I really enjoyed learning how to make a collage. I hope you can come play at my house soon."

Often your friends will do special things for you. At times like that you can return their kindness by thanking them.

If you are generous, you are willing to share whatever you have with your friends.

Kim skipped into the grade one classroom. She was carrying the new pencil box she had gotten for her birthday. Inside were 32 pencil crayons, 12 felt pens and a rainbow eraser.

"This eraser is so pretty, I don't ever want to use it," decided Kim as she set it on the corner of her desk. "I'll use my old pink eraser instead."

Just then Colette tapped Kim on the shoulder. "I made some awful mistakes in my exercise book and I lost my eraser. Could I please use yours?"

"Sure," smiled Kim. She lifted the lid of her desk. Her eraser wasn't there. Kim moved everything around in her desk. The old eraser had disappeared!

"Quick, Kim," urged Colette. "I've got to hand in my book right now."

"I can't find my eraser," said Kim. "I guess it's lost."

Colette noticed the rainbow eraser sitting neatly on the corner of Kim's desk. "May I use that one?"

Kim's face fell. "My **new** eraser? Well, I . . ." Then she saw Colette's hurt expression. She picked up her new eraser and passed it to her friend. "Okay, buddy," she smiled.

"Thanks," said Colette as she hurried back to her desk.

Sometimes it may be difficult to share something that is new or special. It's generous to let your friends use things you would rather keep for yourself.

It is generous to offer to help pay for something.

Jason and Janice were grocery shopping with their mother.

"What kind of cereal would you like?" she asked.

"We get to pick today? Hurrah!" cried Jason.

"Let's get that new crispy corn cereal," suggested Janice.

As they walked up and down the aisles the grocery cart filled quickly. Their mother sighed. "I didn't think we needed so many things. This trip is going to be quite expensive."

Jason looked worried. "Uh, you haven't got Nipper's dog food yet. Is that going to cost lots more?"

"Yes, dog food is fairly pricey. But Nipper does need some more," she said.

Jason and Janice looked thoughtfully at one another. Then Jason dug deep into his pocket.

"I haven't spent my allowance yet." He held out fifty cents. "You can have this."

Janice clicked open her purse shaped like a pony. "You can have my two quarters, Mom."

Jason and Janice's mother leaned down and hugged them. She smiled warmly. "I think I can manage to pay for everything without taking your allowance. But thank you both for offering. That shows me what generous people you are."

Offering to pay for something is unselfish. Even if your offer is not accepted, your willingness to help shows that you have a generous nature.

Being generous means supporting charities and other good causes.

Jason and Janice waited at the door of the store while their mother paid for the groceries.

Janice noticed a man in a wheelchair who was sitting at a special display table nearby.

"Is that man giving out food samples like the lady at the sausage counter?" asked Janice.

"No, he's collecting money to help disabled people," explained Jason.

Janice nodded her head and looked serious. "You mean, for people in wheelchairs and stuff?"

"Yes, for the March of Dimes," said Jason.

Janice looked thoughtfully at the man in the wheelchair. She snapped open her purse and took out her fifty cents.

Jason was surprised, and grabbed her arm as she began walking toward the collection box. "Hey, what are you doing? I thought you were going to the ice-cream shop with me."

"I think I'd rather give my allowance to that man," she said.

Jason heard the clink of her quarters as they dropped into the box. He hesitated a moment, then walked toward the collection box. In dropped his allowance.

"Come on," called their mother. "Groceries are done for this week. Now, you're off for an ice-cream cone, aren't you?"

"No thanks, Mom," replied Janice.

"We changed our minds," said Jason.

Donating to a special fund is very generous because it provides help for those who need it.

Generous people always have the time to help others.

Bobby ran down the front steps two at a time. It had taken him longer to get ready to play baseball than he had expected and he didn't want to be late. As he was hurrying up the street he saw Mr. Corban struggling to carry a large bag into his backyard. Several more bags were sitting on the front lawn.

Bobby stopped. Mr. Corban looked tired and hot. If Bobby gave him a hand carrying the bags, he would be even later for the game and get stuck playing outfield. He thought for a moment and then walked over to his neighbor.

"Do you need some help?" asked Bobby.

Mr. Corban set down the bag he was carrying. "I sure do. I think I filled these bags too full," he replied, breathing heavily. "It took me nearly all day to cut the grass and trim the hedges. Now I want to get these bags of trimmings into the back alley."

"We could carry them together," suggested Bobby, picking up one end of the bag.

"I would appreciate your help."

Soon they had the bags stacked neatly in the alley.

"Thank you," smiled Mr. Corban.

"Anytime," replied Bobby.

He hurried down to the park where his friends were already playing baseball. Sure enough he ended up in the outfield but he didn't mind. In fact Bobby was smiling because he felt great for helping his neighbor.

Taking the time to help your friends, neighbors and relatives will make them happy and will make you feel good.

Being generous means giving more than is expected of you.

Ryan and Paul were walking home from school one afternoon.

"Why don't you come over to my house?" suggested Ryan. "My grandpa gave me some new baseball cards. You'll love my Green Sox cards."

When Paul walked into Ryan's room, it wasn't the baseball cards that caught his eye. "Wow, you still have your Easter basket! I finished eating my stuff a long time ago."

Ryan smiled proudly. "My dad thinks I'm amazing because I only eat one chocolate at a time. I'm good at making candy last."

"Well, I'm not," laughed Paul. "In fact, my stomach is beginning to growl right now just looking at it."

Ryan held out the basket which had six chocolate eggs wrapped in foil left in it. "Here, take one," he offered.

"Mmmm," Paul smacked his lips. "I love these."

Ryan had a chocolate too. It was delicious.

They looked at all of Ryan's baseball cards and then they went into Cameron's room to see his collection.

When it was time for Paul to go home, Ryan went back to his bedroom and scooped up the last four chocolate eggs. "Why don't you take these? You'll need energy for your walk home."

Paul looked surprised. "You'd give your last Easter candy to me?"

Ryan smiled. "Sure. Why not? After all, you're one of my best friends."

Paul munched on the eggs all the way home. He could hardly wait for next Easter so he could give some chocolate eggs to Ryan.

You can often delight your friends by being especially generous.

It is generous to go to extra trouble for others.

Mitchell had been doing odd jobs around the house for weeks. He desperately wanted a beautiful golden baseball glove he had seen in the sporting goods store. His parents had said they would buy it for him if he helped out with extra chores. He had helped rake the yard and had swept the back porch and had done everything else he was asked to do.

Each day that went by he felt closer and closer to getting the glove. He knew he would play baseball better with it. Mitchell thought he would be ready to play on the older kids' team.

At last the day came when his parents said they would get him the glove he wanted. He was so excited. All three of them walked to the store together.

"There it is!" exclaimed Mitchell.

He picked up the glove. It felt cool and smooth. It fit his hand perfectly.

"I can hardly wait to try it out," Mitchell smiled. "Tammy and I will have a great time." Then he remembered that Tammy didn't have a glove. Maybe she would get one for her birthday on Saturday.

He suddenly had an idea. He could give her this glove. She would be so surprised. When Mitchell took the glove to the cash register he said to the clerk, "Please gift wrap this."

"Why?" asked his father.

"I want to give it to Tammy for her birthday," Mitchell explained. "She needs a glove."

"But what about you?" asked his mother.

"I can always work hard to get another one," said Mitchell.

His parents beamed at him. "We're very proud of you."

"Tell you what," said his father, "you can get your own glove now and we'll let you work it off."

"Okay!" cried Mitchell. "Then Tammy and I will both have great gloves!"

Putting extra effort into something for someone else shows that you are generous.

Being generous means thinking of other people's needs.

Tammy was watching her father decorate her birthday cake. It was chocolate and looked like a big baseball glove. She sat licking the mixing spoon as he covered the cake in thick chocolate icing.

Suddenly she had a terrible thought. Mitchell was allergic to chocolate and she had forgotten all about it. He wouldn't be able to enjoy her birthday cake.

Her father noticed her frown. "What's the matter?"

"Mitchell can't eat chocolate, Dad," she explained. "It makes him go all red and puffy."

"Well, we could get him some ice cream or something else instead."

"But he would feel left out," Tammy said. She thought and thought. "I've got an idea," she exclaimed.

Tammy's birthday party was marvelous. She and her friends played lots of games. Then she opened her presents. When she unwrapped the glove from Mitchell, she squealed with delight. "It fits perfectly. Thank you so much, Mitchell."

Mitchell was pleased that all his hard work had made his friend happy. He could hardly wait to play baseball with Tammy.

Then it was time for the birthday cake. Mitchell saw the dark chocolate cake. He knew he wouldn't be able to have any. He felt a little sad.

Tammy turned to Mitchell. "You get a special mini-cake all your own," she said smiling. "The white baseball is just for you."

Mitchell grinned. It was wonderful cake.

Some of your friends' needs may not be the same as yours. Remembering other people's needs shows that you have a generous nature.

Generous people share their talents with others.

Tammy loved her new baseball glove. Her big dream was to be on the school's Little League team when she was in grade one.

"The only hitch is that I have to learn how to catch," sighed Tammy.

"I'll help you," said Mitchell enthusiastically. He wanted to be on the Little League team too. "We'll get better together."

The two friends spent some time throwing the ball, but not even the golden baseball gloves could teach them how to catch.

Colette watched for a while. "I don't know," she teased, "but I think maybe the Little League pitcher will fall off his mound laughing when he sees you two."

Mitchell and Tammy looked so downhearted that Colette was sorry she had said anything.

Just then Dylan walked by. "How are the great ball players?" he asked.

"Not very good," admitted Mitchell.

"We drop the ball a lot more often than we catch it," said Tammy.

"Well, I could give you some pointers," suggested Dylan.

"That would be wonderful," cried Tammy.

"Try it like this, Mitchell," Dylan suggested. "Practice your overhand, Tammy, this way."

Dylan certainly knew what he was doing. Tammy and Mitchell were catching the ball at least as often as they missed. By late afternoon they felt like they were ready to sign up for the major leagues.

"Gee, thanks, Dylan," said Tammy as she went in to get ready for dinner.

"Thanks a lot," added Mitchell, following Tammy.

"It was nice of you to help them," said Colette.

"It was fun," smiled Dylan. "Maybe Mitchell or Tammy will be signing autographs one day."

"They'll have to learn to write first, as well as catch," she laughed. "But if they do become famous, it will be you they have to thank for getting them started."

Helping other people learn what you already know may be hard work but it is always rewarding.

Being generous is important.

It was snack time in Miss Foster's kindergarten class. Hannah and Janice were sitting on either side of Michelle, a three-year-old visitor.

"Our teacher said you are going to come to this kindergarten class next year," said Hannah.

"No, I'm not," muttered Michelle. "I don't want to come here!"

Hannah and Janice looked at each other in surprise. They loved kindergarten, and they couldn't think of any reason why the little girl wouldn't want to be there.

"But you loved play time," pointed out Janice. "You got to be the firefighter, and you liked painting."

Michelle looked as if she was going to cry. "I want to go home."

Miss Foster came up to the girls. "Good, I see Hannah and Janice are ready for snack time. Did you wash your hands?"

"Yes, Miss Foster," chorused Hannah and Janice.

"Why, Michelle, you don't look very happy." Miss Foster knelt down beside the little girl. "Where is your snack?"

"I forgot it," whispered Michelle.

Hannah immediately spoke up. "I have a dish full of strawberries. You can have some, Michelle."

"I've got a peanut butter sandwich and a cheese sandwich," said Janice. "Michelle can choose whichever one she wants."

Miss Foster beamed at them. "What a kind offer."

Michelle's face brightened. "I do like kindergarten," she said. " I want to come here every day!"

Generous people share their time and their belongings with others. Their unselfish behavior makes their friends, family and neighbors feel special. Here are some ways you can be generous:
- Share something that is important to you.
- Offer to help others.
- Be willing to give more than might be expected of you.
- Share your talents.

Printed and bound in U